Do You KNOW?

TV STARS

100 challenging questions about sitcom characters, soap opera villains, heroes and heavies, news anchors and talk show hosts

Guy Robinson

SOURCEBOOKS, INC.®
NAPERVILLE, ILLINOIS

Published by Sourcebooks, Inc.
P.O. Box 4410, Naperville, Illinois 60567-4410
(630) 961-3900
Fax: (630) 961-2168
www.sourcebooks.com

ISBN-13: 978-1-4022-1322-9
ISBN-10: 1-4022-1322-0

Printed and bound in the United States of America
SP 10 9 8 7 6 5 4 3 2 1

Do you remember details of favorite TV shows you haven't seen in years? Can you call up the names of the stars you watched in the 1990s—or even earlier decades—and tell about their careers, maybe even quote their best lines? Good. You're in the right place.

This is a quiz about television stars who stick in the memory: their hits, their misses, the names of their characters and other facts about their shows, their catchphrases, a bit about their private lives, and more.

If you're a TV watcher, you'll probably know just about every name in this book. You'll toss off some of the answers almost without thinking—especially if you've been watching reruns lately, or studying a DVD. But keep your guard up, because it's a sure bet you'll find some questions that'll leave you scratching your head.

So here are 100 questions. Count ten points for each correct answer. Where a question has more than one part, you'll be told how to divide the credit. Here and there you'll find a chance to earn five or ten bonus points, so it's theoretically possible to score more than 1,000. (But you won't!)

Figure your performance this way:

Above 900:	**Spectacular!**
700–899:	A very solid showing
500–699:	Nothing to be ashamed of
Below 500:	Told you it was tough

1. Fill in the missing name on this list of women who've hosted the *Today* show:

   Barbara Walters
   Jane Pauley

   _____

   Katie Couric
   Meredith Viera

2. Bill Cosby has been seen in commercials almost as much as on sitcoms. Which of these products and companies has he pitched?

   a. Jell-O
   b. Kodak
   c. Coca-Cola
   d. Texas Instruments

3. Kathie Lee Gifford and her husband, Frank, share an August 16 birthday. How many years older is Frank?

   a. 10
   b. 13
   c. 20
   d. 23

4. Who hosted *The Daily Show* before Jon Stewart, in the show's first two years?

   a. Craig Kilborn
   b. Stephen Colbert
   c. Jay Leno
   d. Stephen Wright

5. For five points apiece, give:

   a. Judge Wapner's first name _____
   b. Judge Judy's last name _____

6. Which of these TV chefs have never run a restaurant?

a. Paula Deen
b. Ina Garten
c. Emeril Lagasse
d. Rachael Ray
e. Bobby Flay
f. Julia Child

7. Fred Rogers, of *Mister Rogers' Neighborhood*, was an ordained minister. Did you know that? Did you? Yes, you did. But can you say his denomination? Can you?

_____

8. What sitcom star caused a fuss at a Cincinnati–San Diego baseball game in 1990 with her rendition of "The Star-Spangled Banner" and the parody of a ballplayer gesture she made after she finished singing " . . . the home of the brave"?

_____

9. What was the name of Mr. T's character on *The A-Team*?

_____

10. For two points each, name the stars who played:

a. a sloppy sportswriter and a principled pathologist
b. that sloppy sportswriter's secretary and a beer bottler
c. Ritchie's mom and Lou's No. 2 at WJM
d. the Ponderosa patriarch and a colonial commander
e. a compassionate cabby and a lonely divorcé

11. Who was Dorothy Petrillo Zbornak? (Hint: Maude Findlay.)

_____

12. **Uh, remember on *Saturday Night Live* . . . when Chris Farley, uh, played a "motivational speaker"? And he got like all excited and jumped up and down, and stuff? Remember? That was awesome! For five points each:**

    a. What was the character's name? _____

    b. Where did he say he lived? _____

13. **What's Jay Leno's hobby?**

    a. deep sea diving

    b. power walking

    c. antique cars and motorcycles

    d. archery

    e. rare books

14. **What actor, in an episode of a hit sitcom, wore a leather jacket and swim trunks as he water-skied over a shark?**

    _____

15. **After *Star Trek* was cancelled, Leonard Nimoy joined the cast of:**

    a. *Columbo*   c. *The Guiding Light*

    b. *Land of the Giants*   d. *Mission: Impossible*

16. **Who was the woman who sold a lot of Wendy's hamburgers by asking of competitors' burgers, "Where's the beef?"**

    a. Carrie Beller   c. Caren Pellet

    b. Clara Peller   d. Calla Lily

17. **What did the director say to open each episode of *Alfred Hitchcock Presents*?**

    "_____"

18. Just *one* of these TV stars *wasn't* born in Canada. Which?

a. Pamela Anderson
b. Conrad Bain
c. Raymond Burr
d. Tommy Chong
e. Selma Diamond
f. James Doohan
g. Michael J. Fox
h. Lorne Greene
i. Ted Koppel
j. Howie Mandel
k. Mike Myers
1. Jason Priestley
m. Paul Shaffer
n. Jay Silverheels
o. Kiefer Sutherland
p. Alex Trebek

19. What kids' favorite in the days of live TV was pulled off the air for a week after he suggested that young viewers take "those little green pieces of paper" out of Daddy's wallet and send them to him?

_____

20. What British television presenter hosted the American version of the imported game show, *Weakest Link*? (Hint: initials A.R.)

_____

21. Drew Carey is a prominent fan of big-league football and baseball teams of which city?

a. New York
b. Los Angeles
c. Pittsburgh
d. Cleveland

22. Which one of these non-human television VIPs has a star on the Hollywood Walk of Fame?

a. Miss Piggy
b. Kermit the Frog
c. Howdy Doody
d. Mighty Mouse
e. Beavis

23. Quick descriptions of two stars known by stage names. Five points for each one you can identify.

    a. A veteran TV interviewer whose name used to be Lawrence Zeiger. _____

    b. Played a wealthy, manipulative California winemaker on a prime time soap, and her birth name was Sarah Jane Fulks. _____

24. Just one angel served the full original run of *Charlie's Angels*, 1976–81. Which?

    a. Farrah Fawcett   d. Cheryl Ladd
    b. Kate Jackson   e. Shelley Hack
    c. Jaclyn Smith   f. Tanya Roberts

25. "Can two divorced men share an apartment without driving each other crazy?" What two sitcom stars tried to answer this weekly question?

_____

26. Paul Lynde began his very long run on *Hollywood Squares* in 1966. What year did he take over the center square?

    a. 1966
    b. 1968
    c. 1975
    d. 1980

27. What's David Letterman's son's name?

_____

28. Match the star with his former occupation:

a. Geraldo Rivera
b. Perry Como
c. Andy Griffith
d. Jerry Springer
e. Howie Mandel

f. high school teacher
g. mayor
h. lawyer
i. carpet salesman
j. barber

29. On three of his best jobs, he played a Milwaukee hardware store owner, a New England small-town sheriff, and a Chicago crime-solving priest. And you've heard his voice in countless commercials. Name him.

_____

30. Kelly Ripa was a regular on all but one of these. Which?

a. *All My Children*
b. *Touched By an Angel*
c. *Dance Party USA*
d. *Hope & Faith*

31. What did Sonny Bono (*The Sonny & Cher Comedy Hour* and others) and Fred Grandy (Gopher on *The Love Boat*) have in common?

_____

32. Among her series roles: a girl called "Princess," a pharmacist named Ellie, Miriam Welby, an evil nurse named Kate, and the doting mother of a very, very odd adult child. Name her.

_____

33. Name the brother and sister, both actors. Five points each.

a. K.C. played the troublemaker son of a shrink. _____
b. C.C. played the daughter of a morning talk show host. _____

34. How about these actor brothers? Again, five points apiece.

a. One played an AIDS sufferer on *Life Goes On*. _____
b. The other played the deputy communications director on *The West Wing*.

_____

35. Who *wasn't* on the first panel of *The View*?

a. Meredith Viera
b. Star Jones
c. Lisa Ling
d. Debbie Matenopolous
e. Barbara Walters

36. Which subject has Ken Burns *not* covered in a TV documentary series?

a. the American Revolution
b. the Civil War
c. World War II
d. baseball
e. jazz

37. Who learned to handle a stick shift so she could drive a music-making family's tour bus in her starring role on a 1970s series?

_____

38. Who hosted the first incarnation of *Jeopardy*, in the pre-Trebek era?

_____

39. Match the star with his musical instrument:

a. Johnny Carson
b. Dick Smothers
c. Arthur Godfrey
d. Ray Romano
e. Jack Benny

f. string bass
g. piano
h. drums
i. ukulele
j. violin

40. What star played a guy named Sam, who owned the place "where everybody knows your name"?

_____

41. Who wrote books titled *Bouncing Back*, *Enter Talking*, and *Still Talking*?

    a. Joan Rivers
    b. Barbara Walters
    c. Rosie O'Donnell
    d. Sally Jessy Raphael

42. What was the name of Billy Crystal's character on *Soap*?

    a. Joel Houston
    b. Jodie Dallas
    c. Danny Austin
    d. Fernando Davis Jr.

43. Which stars were known for these catchphrases? Two points apiece.

    a. "Bang! Zoom!" _____
    b. "Good night, Chet." _____
    c. "Champagne wishes and caviar dreams." _____
    d. "Well, excu-u-u-use me!" _____
    e. "Stifle!" _____

44. Five more:

    a. "Could it be . . . *Satan*?" _____
    b. "You're fired!" _____
    c. "Afternoon, everybody." _____
    d. "Book 'em, Danno." _____
    e. "I'm coming, Elizabeth!" _____

45. He landed the part of Indiana Jones in the movie *Raiders of the Lost Ark*, but he had just signed for a TV series, playing a Vietnam War vet who'd become a detective in Hawaii, and the network wouldn't let him off the hook. So Harrison Ford got to play the big-screen archeologist instead. Who's the actor and what was the series that kept him from that movie role? (Answer both—no partial credit.)

46. What was the name of John Travolta's character on *Welcome Back, Kotter*? (First and last names, please. Again, no partial credit on this one.)

47. He was a Mouseketeer on *The Mickey Mouse Club*, played the son of a widowed homesteader (Chuck Connors) on *The Rifleman*, then became a pop singer with several hit records ("Cindy's Birthday" was one), and now leads a "vintage dance orchestra." Know him?

48. "It's time once again to look into the future"—meaning the year 2000. On whose late-night show?

49. On what two soap operas did Emmy-winner Peter Hansen play the character Lee Baldwin?

50. Just *one* of these stars *didn't* die while acting in a TV series. Which one? (The others all did go on permanent hiatus, causing scriptwriters to scramble. For those, take five bonus points for each cause of death you can give.)

    a. John Ritter (*8 Simple Rules for Dating My Teenage Daughter*)
    b. Madeline Kahn (*Cosby*)
    c. Jean Stapleton (*Archie Bunker's Place*)
    d. Freddie Prinze (*Chico and the Man*)
    e. Jerry Orbach (*Law & Order: Trial by Jury*)
    f. Phil Hartman (*NewsRadio*)
    g. Will Geer (*The Waltons*)

51. What did Buddy Hackett and Bill Cosby do that Groucho Marx had done earlier?

_____

52. He played Connie Brooks' boss, he played the Mitchells' neighbor, and he played roles on several different shows with Lucy. Who was he?

_____

53. Which exit line is repeated several times in Carol Burnett's closing theme song?

    a. "Goodbye"
    b. "So long"
    c. "See you soon"
    d. "Bye now"

54. What TV star had a long-running second-banana gig, emceed a talent show for a dozen years, and flogged sweepstakes run by American Family Publishers? (Hint: Funk & Wagnall's porch.)

_____

55. What late-night host called the studio band his "posse"?

_____

56. The parents were stars of stage or screen, their offspring all stars of the small screen in their own right. Three points for each of the first two pairs, four for the final one.

    a. Peter Pan's son played Mr. Ewing. _____
    b. George Gershwin's son played Hawkeye. _____
    c. Jane's daughter played Allison Mackenzie. _____

57. He takes credit for writing Jack Paar's legendary introduction of the movie star: "Here they are—Jayne Mansfield." Later, he had several talk shows of his own. Can you name him?

_____

58. What do Edward Asner (*The Mary Tyler Moore Show*, *Lou Grant*), Jane Pauley (*Today*), and Cynthia Watros (*Guiding Light*, *Titus*, *The Drew Carey Show*, *Lost*) have in common? (Hint: Richard Thomas does each of them one better.)

_____

59. For two points each, name the stars who played:

    a. an itinerant gambler in the Old West and a private eye with an answering machine
    b. Dobie's beatnik buddy and a bumbling crewman on the *Minnow*
    c. a con man in a POW camp and the host of a game show concerned with surveys
    d. a TV news writer and a cruise ship captain
    e. the voice of a nearsighted cartoon character and a stranded millionaire

60. Arrange these stars in order of height, shortest to tallest:

   a. Estelle Getty (*The Golden Girls*)
   b. Hervé Villechaize (*Fantasy Island*)
   c. Gary Coleman (*Diff'rent Strokes*)

61. Who's Oprah's best friend?

_____

62. What did the head of the Peanut Gallery, an ABC news co-anchor, and a singer who had her own daytime and evening series have in common?

_____

63. What comic star of the small screen (and the big one) died in his room at the Chateau Marmont, a Los Angeles hotel, on March 5, 1982? (Ten extra points for the name of the person implicated in the death.)

_____

64. Ryan Seacrest was born in:

   a. Oregon
   b. Montana
   c. Florida
   d. Georgia

65. John Hart played the part for a couple of years, but mostly, during the show's long run, another actor portrayed the mysterious man from Texas named Reid. Five points if you can name the character, five more for the name of the star best identified with him.

_____

66. In one episode of *I Love Lucy*, Ricky sang the lyrics to the show's theme song. Here's one stanza with two lines missing. Five points for each one you can provide:

I love Lucy and she loves me,

_____.

Sometimes we quarrel but then,

_____.

67. Michael Delaney Dowd Jr. had his own hit syndicated daytime talk show for years. Who was he?

_____

68. Another brother and sister actor pair, for five points each:

    a. She played Michael J. Fox's sister. _____

    b. He played Ricky Schroeder's best friend. _____

69. Which statement about Cher is untrue?

    a. She didn't graduate from high school.

    b. She has had several tattoos.

    c. She's an Emmy winner.

    d. Her real first name is Dearie.

70. Five more catchphrases. For two points each, who made them popular?

    a. "I pity the fool!" _____

    b. "Did I do that?" _____

    c. "One ringy-dingy, two ringy-dingy. . . ." _____

    d. "Shazbot." _____

    e. "I liked it so much I bought the company." _____

71. Who did the voice of the title character in the series *My Mother, the Car*?

_____

72. Probably no other show has produced as many popular expressions as *Saturday Night Live*. Which of *SNL's* stars is responsible for each of these lines? Two points apiece.

a. "Are you looking at my bum?" _____
b. "And you are . . . ?" _____
c. "Yeah, that's the ticket!" _____
d. "Wouldn't be prudent." _____
e. "Superstar!" _____

73. Yes, *SNL* certainly does give us a lot of catchphrases. Here are five more. For two points each, who said these?

a. "I *hate* when that happens!" _____
b. "That was so funny I forgot to laugh." _____
c. "I'm from Joisey. Are you from Joisey?" _____
d. "I must say." _____
e. "I'm good enough. I'm smart enough. And doggone it, people like me!"
_____

74. What was the name of the 1986-90 series for kids starring Paul Reubens?

_____

75. People who talk on TV for a living fill their airtime with whatever they can think of to talk about, even their pets. For five points apiece, name the departed favored animals owned by:

a. Regis Philbin _____
b. Joan Rivers _____

76. In one episode of *The Partridge Family*, he played a boyfriend of Laurie called Snake, but his TV career didn't hit a high note until he took the part of a guy called Meathead. Who?

_____

77. **For two points apiece, match the TV stars with the titles of their autobiographies:**

    a. *Here We Go Again: My Life in Television*
    b. *To the Stars*
    c. *My First Five Husbands . . . And the Ones Who Got Away*
    d. *Celebrity Detox*
    e. *A Life on the Road*

    f. Rue McLanahan
    g. Rosie O'Donnell
    h. Charles Kuralt
    i. Betty White
    j. George Takei

78. **Do the names of some of her characters lead you to her identity? She's been Stacy Sheridan, Sunny Jo Carrington, Amanda Woodward, and Caitlin Moore. So she's . . .**

    _____

79. **He was best known for his starring role on a children's program that ran for nearly 30 years. But before that, he was the first to play a speechless character on another long-running kids' show. Who was he?**

    _____

80. **They went to the same high school in Jamaica, New York. In the 1990s, each of them landed a starring role in a sitcom, playing characters with their own first names. Her character's last name was Fine, his Barone. Got 'em yet? Five points for each.**

    _____

81. **In a hit sitcom, I played the boss. Then I got my own show playing the same character but in a new job, and this time the show was a drama, not a comedy. Who am I? (Five-point bonus question: In what cities did these shows take place?)**

    _____

82. Who played a character known as J.B. Fletcher?

_____

83. There were five Huxtable kids on *The Cosby Show*. OK, you don't have to name *all* the actors—any three will bring you ten points. Five extra points for name four and ten extra for the fifth, if you're that good.

    a. _____
    b. _____
    c. _____
    d. _____
    e. _____

84. I had a recurring role on a major hit drama series; in one episode my character served as Acting President of the United States for two days. On another series—a smash sitcom that lasted nine seasons—I played a blue-collar husband and father. I've been a multi-repeat guest host on *Saturday Night Live*. Who am I? Figure it out yet?

_____

85. Who regularly led off his program by inviting his audience to "watch the pictures as they fly through the air"?

    a. Joey Bishop
    b. Pat Sajak
    c. Ernie Kovacs
    d. Tom Snyder

86. Who ended each show for years by pleading with his audience: "Help control the pet population. Have your pets spayed or neutered." (Hint: "Here's the first item up for bids.")

_____

87. Can you figure out the identities of these two TV stars, for five points apiece? P.D. portrayed look-alike teenage cousins on her own series in the 1960s; M.G. played a teenager in a frontier family in the 1970s and 1980s. In a 1979 television version of *The Miracle Worker*, M. played Helen Keller to P.'s Annie Sullivan. Each of them has served as president of the Screen Actors Guild. Who are they?

P. D. _____
M. G. _____

88. Five points apiece for naming these two comedy show stars:

a. S.B. first played Arthur's cousin and then got his own show, where he played a domestic. _____
b. J.A. played a messed-up guy who really would have preferred to be an architect or a marine biologist, and also did the voice of an incompetent private detective in an animated sitcom. _____

89. Sure, you know that Sally Field had the title role in *The Flying Nun*, the fantasy sitcom. But do you know what that aerodynamically talented sister's name was?

a. Sister Sixto
b. Sister Jacqueline
c. Sister Bertrille
d. Sister Ana

90. Just one of these statements about *Wheel of Fortune* principals is true. Which?

a. The nighttime show started before the daytime version.
b. Before *Wheel*, Pat Sajak never worked in television.
c. Vanna White is the only wheel turner ever on the shows.
d. Pat Sajak hosted the daytime show longer than Chuck Woolery did.

91. I starred in a series that ran for five seasons, covering much of my teenage years. On the show, I had an older brother (who enjoyed tormenting me) and an older sister (who was enough of a hippie to really tick off my father—but then, he ticked off pretty easily). Each episode began with old home movies and Joe Cocker singing a bit of "With a Little Help from My Friends." Who am I?

_____

92. Who *wasn't* on Johnny Carson's first *Tonight Show*, in 1962?

a. Rudy Vallee
b. Joan Crawford
c. Jerry Lewis
d. Tony Bennett
e. Mel Brooks
f. Groucho Marx

93. I did a kids' show about a cartoon character and his dog, on which I showed viewers how to put a "Magic Drawing Screen" (OK, OK—it was just a clear plastic sheet) over the TV screen so they could play connect-the-dots and otherwise draw on it with a crayon. I also hosted a show that had a panel of kids answering questions, and another with a panel of octogenarians. And I emceed a program that was caught up in the 1950s quiz show scandals, big time. Who am I?

_____

94. A pair of married couples. Figure them out for five points per couple.

a. He played an impossibly amoral New York taxi dispatcher, she a Boston bar waitress who was twice married and perpetually unlucky with men.

_____

b. He was a piano-playing late-show host, she a game-show panelist whose sister was forever being threatened with a trip to the moon.

_____

95. What do Arthur Spooner and Frank Costanza have in common?

_____

96. Match the newscasters and faux-newscasters with their signoffs:

a. "And that's the way it is."
b. "Courage."
c. "So it goes."
d. "That's the news and I am outta here."
e. "Good night and good news."

f. Dennis Miller ("Weekend Update" on *Saturday Night Live*)
g. Linda Ellerbee (*NBC News Overnight* and others)
h. Walter Cronkite (*CBS Evening News*)
i. Ted Baxter (*The Mary Tyler Moore Show*)
j. Dan Rather (*CBS Evening News*)

97. For years, Bert Parks hosted the yearly Miss America pageant. He also had a long career in early daytime television. Which of these shows *didn't* make it onto his résumé?

a. *The Big Payoff*
b. *Break the Bank*

c. *Yours for a Song*
d. *Queen for a Day*

98. Five points for the names used in each of these two *Saturday Night Live* recurring music bits:

a. Adam Sandler's cape-wearing, aria-singing character _____
b. The lounge singers (Jan Hooks and Nora Dunn) whose set always included "Clang, clang, clang went the trolley . . .") _____

99. Erik Estrada, who played the California Highway Patrol officer known as "Ponch" (*CHiPs*), was born in:

a. Puerto Rico
b. Mexico

c. New York
d. Kansas

100. Leonard Nimoy's first autobiography was titled *I Am Not Spock*. Twenty years later, he published another. What did he call the second one?

_____

ANSWERS

1. Deborah Norville (1990–91)

2. All of them

3. d.

4. a.

5. a. Joseph (*The People's Court*), b. Scheindlin (*Judge Judy*)

6. b., d., and f.

7. Presbyterian

8. Roseanne Barr

9. B.A. (for Bad Attitude, so they say) Baracus

10. a. Jack Klugman (*The Odd Couple, Quincy*), b. Penny Marshall (*The Odd Couple, Laverne & Shirley*), c. Mary Tyler Moore (*The Dick Van Dyke Show, The Mary Tyler Moore Show*), d. Lorne Greene (*Bonanza, Battlestar Gallactica*), e. Judd Hirsch (*Taxi, Dear John*)

11. Bea Arthur's character on *The Golden Girls* (she played Ms. Findlay on *Maude* and, earlier, on *All in the Family*)

12. a. Matt Foley, b. "in a *van . . . down by the river!*"

13. c.

14. Henry Winkler (as the Fonz on *Happy Days*)

15. d. (playing the part of "The Great Paris")

16. b.

17. "Good e-e-e-vening."

18. i. (born in England)

19. Soupy Sales

20. Anne Robinson

21. d.

22. b.

23. a. Larry King (*Larry King Live*), b. Jane Wyman (*Falcon Crest*)

24. c. (as Kelly)

25. Tony Randall and Jack Klugman (Felix and Oscar in *The Odd Couple*)

26. b.

27. Harry

28. a.-h., b.-j., c.-f., d.-g., e.-i.

29. Tom Bosley (Mr. Cunningham on *Happy Days*, Sheriff Amos Tupper of Cabot Cove, Maine on *Murder, She Wrote*, and Father Frank Dowling on *Father Dowling Mysteries*)

30. b.

31. Both became Republican members of the U.S. House of Representatives

32. Elinor Donahue (*Father Knows Best*, *The Andy Griffith Show*, *The Odd Couple*, *Days of Our Lives*, *Get a Life*)

33. The Camerons: a. Kirk (Mike Seaver on *Growing Pains*), b. baby sister Candace (D.J. Tanner on *Full House*)

34. The Lowes: a. Chad (Jesse on *Life Goes On*), b. older brother Rob (Sam Seaborn on *The West Wing*)

35. c.

36. a.

37. Shirley Jones (as the materfamilias on *The Partridge Family*)

38. Art Fleming

39. a.-h., b.-f., c.-i., d.-g., e.-j.

40. Ted Danson (Sam Malone on *Cheers*)

41. a.

42. b.

43. a. Jackie Gleason (*The Honeymooners*), b. David Brinkley (*The Huntley-Brinkley Report*—the response from Chet Huntley, of course, was "Good night, David. And good night for NBC News"), c. Robin Leach (*Lifestyles of the Rich and Famous*), d. Steve Martin (*Saturday Night Live*),
e. Carroll O'Connor (*All in the Family*)

44. a. Dana Carvey (*Saturday Night Live*), b. Donald Trump (*The Apprentice*), c. George Wendt (*Cheers*), d. Jack Lord (*Hawaii Five-O*), e. Redd Foxx (*Sanford and Son*)

45. Tom Selleck, *Magnum, P.I.*

46. Vinnie Barbarino

47. Johnny Crawford

48. Conan O'Brien's

49. *General Hospital* and *Port Charles*

50. c. The script said Edith Bunker died of a stroke, but Jean Stapleton had simply left the show, very much alive (bonus: a. heart problem, b. ovarian cancer, d. shot himself, e. prostate cancer,
f. murdered by his wife, g. respiratory failure)

51. Emcee the quiz show *You Bet Your Life*

52. Gale Gordon (*Our Miss Brooks*, *Dennis the Menace*, and all those Lucy shows)

53. b. (The song, "It's Time to Say So Long," was written by her husband and producer, Joe Hamilton)

54. Ed McMahon (*The Tonight Show Starring Johnny Carson*, *Star Search*)

55. Arsenio Hall (*The Arsenio Hall Show*)

56. a. Mary Martin and her son Larry Hagman (*Dallas*), b. Robert Alda (*Rhapsody in Blue*) and his son Alan Alda (*M*A*S*H*), c. Maureen O'Sullivan (*Tarzan the Ape Man* and others) and her daughter Mia Farrow (*Peyton Place*)

57. Dick Cavett

58. Each is the parent of twins (Thomas, of *The Waltons*, has triplets)

59. a. James Garner (*Maverick* and *The Rockford Files*), b. Bob Denver (*The Many Loves of Dobie Gillis* and *Gilligan's Island*), c. Richard Dawson (*Hogan's Heroes* and *Family Feud*), d. Gavin MacLeod (*The Mary Tyler Moore Show* and *The Love Boat*), and e. Jim Backus (*Mr. Magoo* and *Gilligan's Island*)

60. b. (3'11"), c. (4'8"), a. (4'11")

61. Gayle King (who was a local news anchor and had her own talk show before she started working for Oprah's magazine and *The Oprah Winfrey Show*)

62. The surname Smith (Buffalo Bob Smith on *Howdy Doody*, Howard K. Smith on *ABC Evening News*, and Kate Smith on *The Kate Smith Hour* and *The Kate Smith Evening Hour*)

63. John Belushi (extra points: Cathy Smith, who served jail time for involuntary manslaughter after she was convicted of having injected him with a combination of cocaine and heroin)

64. d.

65. For most of *The Lone Ranger*'s run, Clayton Moore starred

66. I love Lucy and she loves me,
We're as happy as two can be.
Sometimes we quarrel but then,
How we love making up again.

67. Mike Douglas (*The Mike Douglas Show*)

68. The Bateman siblings: a. Justine (*Family Ties*), b. kid brother Jason (*Silver Spoons*)

69. d.

70. a. Mr. T. (*The A-Team*), b. Jaleel White (*Family Matters*), c. Lily Tomlin (*Rowan and Martin's Laugh-In*), d. Robin Williams (*Mork and Mindy*), e. Victor Kiam (commercials for Remington electric razors)

71. Ann Sothern

72. a. Mike Myers (as Simon), b. David Spade (as Dick Clark's receptionist), c. Jon Lovitz (as Tommy Flanagan), d. Dana Carvey (as George Bush Sr.), e. Molly Shannon (as Mary Katherine Gallagher)

73. a. Billy Crystal (as Willie the night watchman), b. Gilda Radner (as Lisa Loopner), c. Joe Piscopo (as Paulie Herman), d. Martin Short (as Ed Grimley), e. Al Franken (as Stuart Smiley)

74. *Pee-wee's Playhouse*

75. a. Joan's Yorkie was Spike, b. the Philbin family cat was Ashley

76. Rob Reiner (Mike Stivic on *All in the Family*)

77. a.-i., b.-j., c.-f., d.-g., e.-h.

78. Heather Locklear

79. Bob Keeshan (the Captain on *Captain Kangaroo* and the first Clarabell the Clown on *Howdy Doody*)

80. Fran Drescher (Fran Fine on *The Nanny*), Ray Romano (Ray Barone on *Everybody Loves Raymond*)

81. Ed Asner, Lou Grant on *The Mary Tyler Moore Show* and *Lou Grant* (bonus: Minneapolis and Los Angeles)

82. Angela Lansbury (on *Murder, She Wrote*, as crime-solving writer Jessica Fletcher, whose mystery novels were published with just the initials)

83. Sabrina Le Beauf (Sondra), Lisa Bonet (Denise), Malcolm-Jamal Warner (Theo), Tempestt Bledsoe (Vanessa), and Keshia Knight Pulliam (Rudy)

84. John Goodman (*The West Wing, Roseanne*)

85. d. (*The Tomorrow Show*)

86. Bob Barker (*The Price Is Right*)

87. Patty Duke (*The Patty Duke Show*) and Melissa Gilbert (*Little House on the Prairie*)

88. a. Scott Baio (*Happy Days* and *Joanie Loves Chachi, Charles in Charge*), b. Jason Alexander (*Seinfeld, Duckman*)

89. c.

90. d.

91. Fred Savage (*The Wonder Years*)

92. c. (Groucho introduced Johnny, Tony sang "I Left My Heart in San Francisco," the Phoenix Singers folk trio performed, and, yes, Ed was at the far end of the couch)

93. Jack Barry (*Winky Dink and You, Juvenile Jury, Life Begins at Eighty, Twenty-One*)

94. a. Danny DeVito (*Taxi*) and wife Rhea Pearlman (*Cheers*), b. Steve Allen (*The Tonight Show*) and wife Jayne Meadows (*I've Got a Secret*, sister of Audrey Meadows, Alice Kramden on *The Honeymooners*)

95. Both characters—Carrie's father on *The King of Queens* and George's father on *Seinfeld*— were played by Jerry Stiller

96. a.-h., b.-j., c.-g., d.-f., e.-i.

97. d. (that was Jack Bailey's show)

98. a. Opera Man, b. the Sweeney Sisters

99. c.

100. *I Am Spock*